SEVILLE

Most of the proper names in the guide have been left in spanish to enable the visitor to refer to signs and plans in that
lenguage and fix his position.

A few useful words to bear in mind: Capilla, (chapel), museo
(museum), palacio (palace), parque (park), torre (tower).

Published by EDILUX S.L.
Editor: J. Agustín Núñez
Original text: Edilux S.L.
English translation: John Shilling
Photographs: Miguel Román and J. Agustín Núñez
Photographic composition: EDILUX S.L.
Layout, design: Estrella Román
Drawings: Pablo Román
Printing: Copartgraf s.c.a.
Binding: Hermanos Olmedo s.l.
ISBN: 84-87282-41-5
L.D.: GR-736/2001

© EDILUX S.L.
E-Mail: ediluxsl@supercable.es

SEVILLE
in focus

S eville was founded and Christened 'Hispalis' by the Phoenicians approximately 28 centuries ago in the depression formed by the lower Guadalquivir, and about 100km from its mouth. The river has determined the city's history: thanks to the fertility of the land, easy access by water and its strategic position overlooking the fertile Andalusian plains, it became a Tartessian centre and a coveted Carthaginian colony which the Romans used as a theatre for their military operations. In 205 BC Scipio founded Itálica over which Caesar and Pompey fought for control and where the emperors Trajan and Hadrian were born. The Vandals, who gave their name to the whole region, conquered and destroyed it, and the Visigoths chose it as the base for their civil wars against Toledo in the 6th century. The Muslims renamed it Yzvilia and it played an all-important role in the first three centuries of Cordovan rule. It was devastated by the Vikings in 844, but later became the most important of the independent Taifa kingdoms (1023), even aspiring to the inheritance of the Caliphate. The Sevillian sultan Al-Mutamid, under Christian threat from Alfonso VI, asked the help of the Almoravids (1090), concious that he was changing the course of the history of al-Andalus. Later in 1146, the Almohads arrived, made Seville their capital and built the Giralda (1198). Fifty years later, the Christians led by Fernando III also chose it as their base. From 1504 to 1717 it held the monopoly of trade with the Americas, was the first city in Europe, the world centre for the gold trade and a showpiece of civilization and culture. The singular heritage of today's Seville is a direct result of such a colourful history.

HOW TO USE THIS GUIDE

This guidebook is organised around short routes and walks around the historic city centre. It starts with a little history.

LAY-OUT OF EACH CHAPTER

Name of the area

Introduction and general information

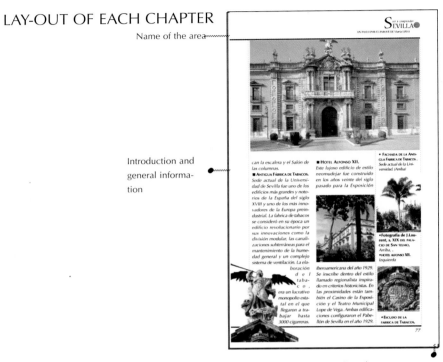

Complementary texts

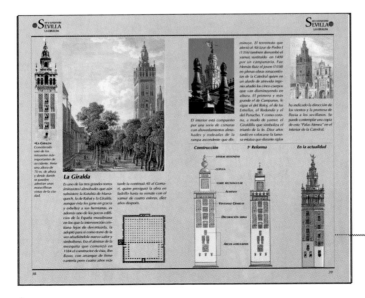

Drawings and plans of the city monuments

CONTENTS

The History of Seville
Ancient Seville   8

Seville and its monuments
Plan of the historic
centre   16

Walk around the Plaza del Triunfo
Cathedral   *20*
Giralda   40
Reales Alcázares   42

Walk through the Santa Cruz district
Casa de Pilatos   64

Other places of interest
The Town Hall   72
La Torre del Oro   74
El Museo de Bellas Artes   76
El Hospital de la Caridad   80
La Plaza de Toros de la
Maestranza   82

A walk to the María Luisa Park.
El Palacio de San Telmo 86
La Antigua Fábrica de
Tabacos   87
El Parque de María Luisa 88

The Iberoamerican Exposition (1929)   92
La Plaza de España   92
La Plaza de América   98

Fiestas and Popular traditions.   110
The Abril fair   114

A walk around the Cartuja Island
El Palenque   120
El Auditorio   120
El Puente de la Barqueta

A tour through the province of Seville
Carmona   130
Ecija   132
Estepa   134
Osuna   134
Bollullos de la Mitación 138

Itálica   140

Plan of Seville   142

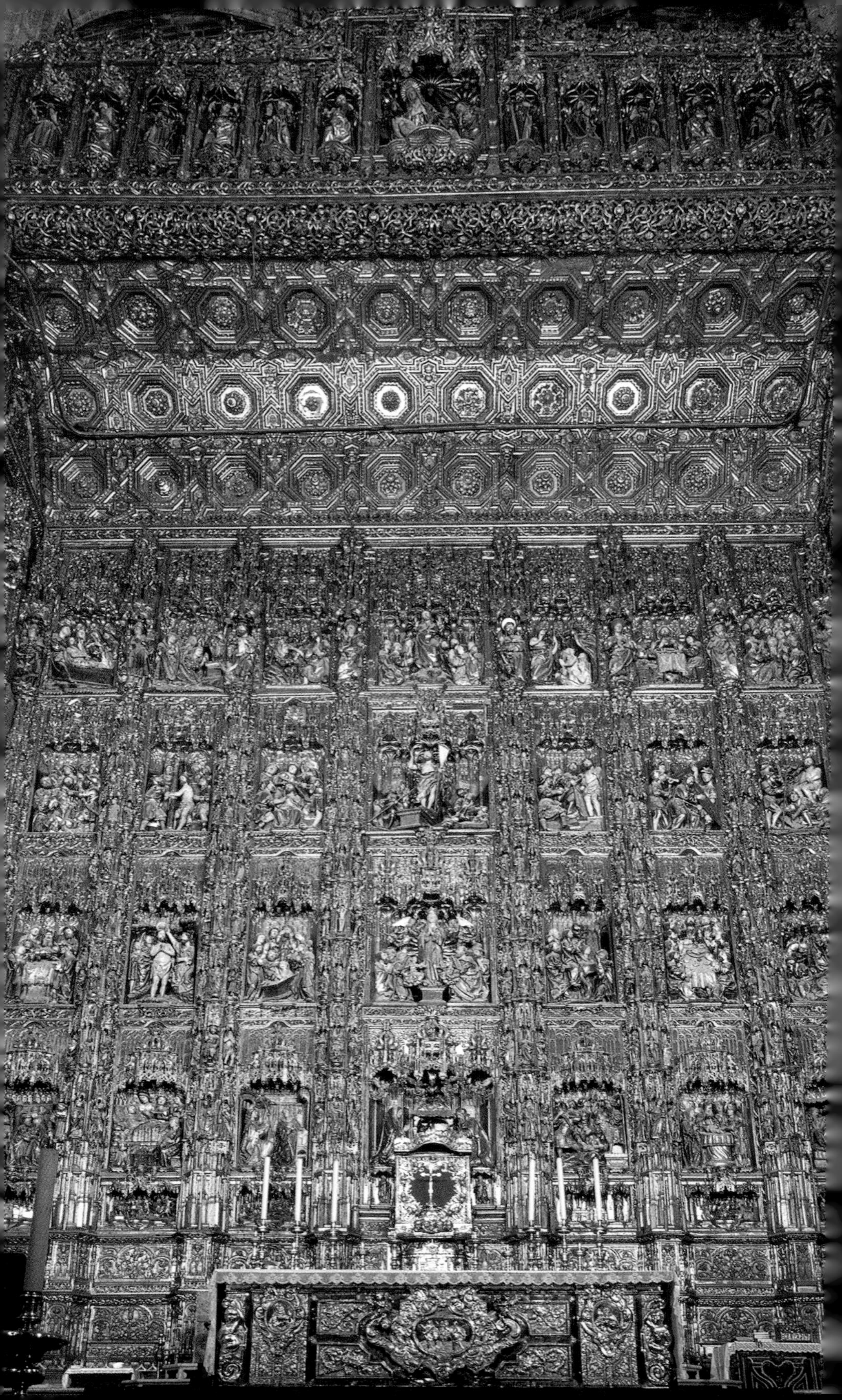

SEVILLE
in focus

The History of Seville
Seville and its monuments

• **VEIW BY WYNGAER-DEN.** *The spectacular growth of the city can be seen in this drawing by the Flemish artist Anton van den Wyngaerden and dating from the reign of Philip II. Wyngaerden, the least known of the artist-travellers of the 16th century, was the best graphic recorder of his time, leaving us detailed townscape views of all the principal cities of Spain. Here, depicting Seville, and in spite of a certain idealized air, the accuracy of the drawing is evident, even in the details.*

The History of Seville

For centuries the city of Seville served as a gateway from the river Guadalquivir to the hinterland of the peninsula, and used by the great eastern civilizations entering in search of precious metals and trade.

■ Ancient Seville
Tartessus

The history of Seville starts 28 centuries ago at that point where the river ceases to be navigable, on a mound between 8 and 16m high with little risk from the frequent floods. It was the river port used to ship the mineral wealth of the Sierra Morena mountains for the Mediterranean trade, dominated by the Phoenicians and Greeks. And it is from the Greeks that we first hear of the mythical kingdom of Tartessus, the real existance and culture of which was confirmed by the discovery of the fabulous Carambobo treasure.

The elaborate designs are evidence of an advanced civilization.

■ Romans

The struggle for hegemony in the Mediterranean was fought out between the Carthaginians and the Romans, with the latter, after

winning the Punic Wars, finally imposing their dominion over the whole sea.

In 206 BC., a little to the north of the present city, the victorious general Scipio Africanus founded a colony called Itálica for his veterans. It was to be the birthplace of the emperors Trajan and Hadrian. Caesar,victor at Munda of the civil war with Pompey, captured Hispalis in 45 BC, refounding it as a colony and giving it a name for the first time. With the pax Romana of Augustus, Seville became one of the most important cities in the empire, engaging in more trade than even Cordova, the capital of Bética.

■ Visigoths

The decadence of Rome after the beginning of the 5th century closed an era of splendour for Seville until the coming of the Visigoths, even though these also used it as a centre for their in-

fighting. With the conversion to Christianity of their king in 589 the city once again became the centre of religious and political life and counted such important figures as St. Leandro and St. Isidoro, the latter author of 'Ethymologiae', an ambitious encyclopedia of contemporary knowledge in all fields.

■ Seville under the Muslims

Once again Seville became the chosen city for invaders, this time the Muslims, a great number of them settling here after the conquest of 711. Although shortly afterwards they moved the capital of the Omayyad emirate to Cor-dova, Seville remained influencial due to the power of family clans, mostly Yeme-nites. This lasted until Abderrahman I (756-788), who had counted on the clans to achieve inde-

●ALAMEDA DE HÉRCULES.
phot. by J. Laurent.
The old Chronicles claim that one of the most popular heroes of mythology, Hercules, indicated with six stone pillars, the site where Julius Caesar would found the city of Seville. The present columns with their impressive statues by Diego de Pesquera, were set up in the newly formed Alameda or avenue of Hercules in the 16th century as a homage to the founders of the city. The columns and capitals come from the Roman temple in Mármoles street.

Seville was conquered in 712 by Musa ibn Nasayr and for the next five centuries of Muslim rule played a major role in the politics and culture of the country.

pendence from Damascus, began to use mercenaries in a drive to create political unity. It was the success of these policies which eventually led to the creation of an independent Caliphate (929).

A hundred years later the Caliphate collapsed (1031), and Seville became the most important of the small kingdoms or 'Taifas' which emerged from the ruins. Some of the poet-kings of the Abbadid ruling dynasty even attempted to restore the Caliphate, believing themselves to be its true heirs. Under pressure from the Christian king Alfonso VI who had captured Toledo in 1085, the best known of these Abbadid poet-kings, al-Mutamid (1068-1090), appealed for help to Almoravids of North Africa.

Their leader, Yusuf ibn Tashfin, not only halted the Christians, but he then deposed the Abbadids and made himself master of Seville in 1091. A second invasion from North Africa, in 1147, left the Almohads in power. These made

Ysvilia their capital and set about restoring and beautifying it, and enlarging it with a new city wall

(on which is the Torre del Oro, 1221) linking the port and Alcázar or fort. Their greatest work however, was the building of the Great Friday Mosque which has the Giralda as a minaret. It was under the hundred-year rule of the Almohads that Seville became a truly great city, with the medieval urban structure that has survived to this day.

■ **Medieval Seville**

Five years after Fernando III, the Holy, had conquered the city (1248), his son Alfonso X, the Wise, made his much loved Seville a royal seat taking up almost permanent residence in his favourite city. Making the best of damage

• **THE WEDDING BULLFIGHT.** *Miniatures from the manuscript, 'Songs to Holy Mary' by Alfonso X, the Wise.*

caused by an earthquake, Pedro I, the Cruel, reconstructed the Reales Alcázares, thereby giving birth to the mudéjar style. The story of Seville in the 15th century is largely taken up with the colossal undertaking of building the Cathedral, which started in 1401 and continued until 1511. At the close of the century, with Granada conquered by the Catholic Monarchs and the discovery of America by Columbus, the future of Seville was about change once more.

Although Seville was always a favourite with Spanish royalty, Alfonso X together with his father Fernando III and Pedro I, are the monarchs most closely identified with the city.

Above left, engraving by Hoefnagel delightfully capturing the bucolic charms of rural Seville.

• CHRISTOPHER COLUMBUS

Columbus was associated with Seville from 1492, when he first sailed to the New World. Although he died in Valladolid, he was buried on the Caribbean island of Santo Domingo until his remains were removed to Cuba. After Cuba became independent, the government decided to bring him back to Spain, and he was finally laid to rest in Seville.

■ MODERN TIMES IN SEVILLE

The reconquest of Granada in 1492 by the Catholic Monarchs, Isabella I and Ferdinand V, and the discovery of America by Christopher Columbus in the same year marked the birth of a new era, of modern times, for the city. Seville entered a new golden age, the most important in all its history, when it became the

centre for Spanish trade with its American possessions (1503). This privileged position was maintained for over 200 years. It is understand-able, then, that the population of the city grew spectacularly in a short period of time and that Seville soon became one of the most important cities in Europe. When the Hapsburg dynasty gained the throne and Charles V became the head of the Holy Roman Empire, Seville was the financial heart of Europe, the port of arrival for the immense wealth of the Americas. These riches were to sustain the religious and political struggles waged during the sixteenth century by Charles and his son, Philip II, for the

• **MIGUEL DE CER-VANTES** *The immortal Spanish author is closely linked to Seville. This is the city where he lived, where he wrote "Novelas ejemplares", and also in which he was imprisoned.*
Ayuntamiento, top left, built in 1527 to the design of the architect Diego de Riaño, and one of the finest examples of the Plateresque style.
Below, detail of the south front.

Spanish domination of Europe. Spain suffered a period of economic and institutional crisis during the following century, with the decadence of the monarchy and the terrible plagues of 1649 that ravaged town and country, including Seville. The eighteenth century saw the War of Succession that divided Spain, and in 1717 a serious blow to Seville: the loss of her privileged monopoly over trade with the Americas. This passed to Cadiz, for practical reasons, the Atlantic port being able to accommodate much larger ships. This stage of economic decline coincided, however, with an important cultural and artistic revival. Seville, during the first half of the seventeenth century, was home to artists such as Veláz-quez, Zurbarán, Alonso Cano, Murillo, and Miguel Cervantes. Schools of religious painting were founded, whose character impregnated the city. With the accession of the Bourbon dynasty, supported by Seville during the War of the Spanish Succession, there followed a period of economic recovery. This prosperous period continued until the disastrous Lisbon earthquake of 1755.

- **THE FAMOUS WHITE DOVES** *in the Parque María Luisa.*

•**GUSTAVO ADOLFO BÉCQUER.**
This monument to the famous romantic poet overlooks one of the intersections in the Park, and is flanked by female figures representing different aspects of love. The group stands in the shade of an enormous old cypress tree that lends a certain air of drama to the scene, very much to the taste of the mid-nineteenth century.

■ **SEVILLE FROM THE 19TH TO THE 21ST CENTURY**
Notable events of the mid-nineteenth century in Seville included the founding of the famous cattle fair by a Catalan and a Basque, and the demolition of the walls surrounding the city. The Infanta (Princess) María Luisa donated the park that bears her name, which provided a much needed green

Costumbres Andaluzas.

La Feria de Sevilla

space in the city centre and comprises a romantic landmark. Little by little, the Seville we see today came into being. After the traumatic loss of Spain's colonies in 1898, Seville contemplated her his-

sons. The political scene did not change until after Franco's death in 1975, when democracy was restored The history of Seville during the last twenty years of the twentieth century is marked by another inter-

•THE MARIA LUISA PARK
Each corner and area of the Park forms an integral part of the city and its history: the famous white doves,

toric legacy as a source of inspiration for the future and was chosen, jointly with Barcelona, to host the great Spanish-American exhibition held in 1929. Although this did not provide the hoped-for economic and industrial boost, it did alleviate many of the chronic deficiencies of the city and provided the infrastructure necessary for modernisation. After the Spanish Civil War, the whole country suffered an economic recession, aggravated by the international ostracism of General Franco's regime. Many emigrated, for political and economic rea-

national exhibition, Expo '92, which considerably changed the appearance of the city, providing it with a modern infrastructure and services.
Although not all the city's ambitions were realised, it is now firmly established as the administrative capital of the autonomous region of Andalusia and has great promise for future development.

the Neo-Mudejar pavilion (above), the modern railway stations and the airport. The construction and engineering projects of the late twentieth century continue the Seville tradition of audacious design and daring creators.

15

Seville and its Monuments

The present-day city of Seville is an accretion of all the Mediterranean civilizations which have left their mark here, and reflects the history and culture of Spain itself.

⑨ PLAZA DE ESPAÑA
Plza de España.
This is one of the landmarks of the 1929 Exhibition, by which Seville is instantly recognisable.

④ AYUNTAMIENTO (*Town Hall*).
Plaza de San Francisco.
A Renaissance building with plateresque decoration, situated between the plazas San Francisco and Nueva and the hub of Sevillian life.

⑩ MUSEO DE BELLAS ARTES.
Alfonso XII street.
Housed in the old Convento de la Merced and, after the Prado, the most important picture gallery in Spain.

⑫ EL HOSPITAL DE LA CARIDAD
Calle Temprado. Of the many examples of Baroque architecture in Seville, the most representative.

⑪ FABRICA DE TABACO. *The former Tobacco factory, built in the eighteenth century and the present headquarters of Seville University*

CASA DE PILATOS. *Plaza de Pilatos*

This sumptuous palace complex was built by Fadrique Enríquez de Ribera, the first Marquess of Tarifa, on his return from a journey to Jerusalem in 1519. He also introduced the Renaissance style into Seville's civil architecture and possibly, by his adoption of the Via Crucis, inspired the Holy Week processions in the city.

② ARCHBISHOP'S PALACE. This is one of the most important Baroque constructions in Seville and dates from the sixteenth century.

① THE CATHEDRAL

Plza. Virgen de los Reyes.

The third largest in the world, the cathedral in Seville was built on the site of the former mosque, of which some elements still remain, such as the Patio de los Naranjos and the Giralda. The Cathedral is Gothic.

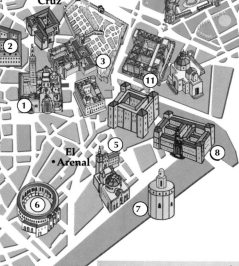

③ LOS REALES ALCÁZARES
Plaza del Triunfo.

⑥ THE MAESTRANZA BULLRING
A landmark of Seville.

⑧ PALACIO DE SAN TELMO
Avda de Roma.

SEVILLE

in focus

(Around the Plaza del Triunfo)
Seville Cathedral
The Giralda tower
Reales Alcázares (the Royal Fortress)

The Cathedral of Seville

After the conquest in 1248, the old mosque was consecrated and for 153 years kept in use as a Christian cathedral. It was common in those times to take over the mosques in this way. The only survivors of this mosque are the Patio de los Naranjos and the converted minaret and symbol of the city, the Giralda.

In the early 15th century, the ecclesiastical authorities decided to build a cathedral on the site of the Moorish mosque, a cathedral of such dimensions that "when they contemplate it, future generations will think us demented". Today, it is one of the largest cathedral in the Christian world.

The admiration of the Christian conquerors for Islamic art did not extend to the mosques, which were normally 'baptised' or simply demolished and replaced by churches. This had also been done with the former Romanesque churches. The geographic and political role of Seville in the 14th and 15th centuries, due to its proximity to the sea and to the Moorish kingdom of Granada, made it the focal point of the Kingdom of Castille. The earthquake of 1366 was the pretext for the construction of the third largest cathedral in the Christian world, a temple so wondrous that "when they contemplate it, future generations will think us demented". In 1401 the tracery work was begun; we do not know the identity of the artist because a subsequent fire destroyed all the papers referring to the construction. Work lasted over a hundred years, under the direction, towards the end of the century, of masters such as Simon of Cologne, Alonso

Rodríguez and the prolific Juan Gil de Hontañón. The style of the cathedral is pure late Gothic: the imposing ver-

ticality of the rhomboidal pillars rising into the ribs of the domes does not detract from the spacious sensation created by the five aisles or create any discordant tension, but rather complements the diaphanous, open atmosphere achieved. The simplicity of line is archetypal Gothic, indeed almost archaic, but over the years additions were made, with the result that the cathedral of Seville is the most important artistic complex in the city, with all genres and styles represented. The first significant revision was that of the original cupola which collapsed and which Hontañón replaced in 1511 with a splendid ribbed dome. The high altar of the chancel, the largest in the Christian world, measuring 360 square metres, with 44 reliefs and over 1000 figures describing the life of Christ, required more than a hundred years for the first phase to be completed. The original style was the Gothic of Dancart, but this later evol-ved to the Renaissance of Jorge Fernández (1525) and finally to the delicate gold leaf work of Alejo Fernández.

The principal grille was the work of the greatest iron-

workers of the age, Bartolomé de Jaén and Friar Francisco de Salamanca

(1518-1529). The latter was also responsible for the grille of the Choir, with its 117 stalls and two magnificent organs, built in an uncom-

• **THE GIRALDA**
This was built by Ahmed ibn Baso and Ali de Gomera for the Caliph Abu Yacub Yusuf in the middle of the 12th century. The minaret was formerly capped with golden spheres on a pinnacle built to commemorate the battle of Alarcos. It was destroyed by an earthquake and the Cathedral Chapter commissioned a turret-belfry from Hernán Ruiz II to replace it. On top he put the 'Giraldillo', a statue which acts as a weather vane and gives the tower its name.

On the left, the Patio de los Naranjos, the former ablutions courtyard and a survivor of the original mosque.

• INTERIOR OF THE CATHEDRAL

The four aisles, nave and many side chapels are supported by sixty columns. The Renaissance Sacristía Mayor, designed in 1528, houses the famous Alfonsine Tables. Right, detail of one of the side doors. Below, the tomb of Columbus, whose remains were brought to Seville from Valladolid in the crisis year of 1898 after having travelled from Santo Domingo via Cuba.

promising Baroque by Duque Cornejo. The Cathe-dral occupies the entire site of the

former mosque except what used to be the ablutions courtyard. It is a monumental construction with a nave, four

aisles, side chapels, a transept and an apse, all contained within the main walls. In consequence, there lacks a sense of directionality inside the structure; there is no ambulatory as such, but rather spaces that have been added in which chapels and sacristies have been inserted. External buttresses and abutments have been applied to a proudly fashioned stone block, in contrast to and affirming itself over the Islamic brickwork it has replaced.

The Capilla Real, behind the Capilla Mayor, holds the intact remains of St Ferdinand in a Baroque silver urn, together with those of his son Alfonso X the Wise and the latter's wife, Beatrice of Swabia. The Chapel is Renaissance, by Gaínza (1551), although the dome was the work of the Cordoban artist Hernán Ruiz II. Presiding the altarpiece is the Virgin of the Kings (13th century), much loved in Seville. This figure was created in a French workshop, apparently a gift from his cousin Louis IX (Saint Louis), King of France, to the conqueror of Seville.

The importance of the Cathedral Chapter is evident in the sumptuous chambers, and especially in the SACRISTIA MAYOR (1528-1543), crowned by a dome designed by Riaño and Gaínza, possibly with the intervention of Diego de Siloé. Here we can see the magnificent 'Descent from the Cross' by Campagna, the paintings of San Isidro and San Leandro by Murillo, one of the most beautiful monstrances created by

Arce and the Alphonsine Tryptic on Panels. THE SACRISTIA DE LOS CÁLICES, in Gothic style by Alonso Rodríguez, is presided over by Goya's painting of Santa Justa and Santa Rufina, the patron saints of Seville. Also hung

here are pictures by Valdés Leal, Zurbarán's 'Virgin and Child', and 'St John the Baptist'. There are four panels

by Alejo Fernández.
The Antechamber and the Chapter House by Hernán Ruiz the Younger have breath-

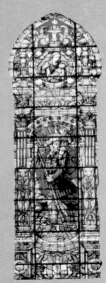

• THE MAIN GRILLE is the work of Bartolomé de Jaén and Francisco de Salamanca (1518-29). The stained glass windows (below) mark the beginning of a golden age in Spanish glass-work.

•EL CRISTO DE LA CLEMENCIA, left, was carved in wood by Martínez Montañés. It measures nearly 2m.

• **CAPILLA MAYOR**
Detail of the altar. Opposite and following pages views of the Cathedral.

• **VIDRIERA**
stained-glass window by Enrique Alemán who seems to have modelled this figure on Charles V.

taking domes and floors, but equally impressive are the treasures within the other chapels: the "VIRGEN DE LA ANTIGUA" chapel, the sailor's

same name, an unusual subject for the painter. La CAPILLA DE SAN PEDRO contains canvases by Zurbarán, painted expressly for the chapel.

haven, the monument to Cardinal Mendoza by Domenico A. Fancelli; the CAPILLA BAUTISMAL with 'The Vision of St Anthony' by Murillo, a painting that was stolen but later recovered. The CAPILLA DE SCALAS has 'The Virgin of Granada' from the workshop of the Della Robbia family. Alonso Cano painted a sweet-faced Virgin of Bethlehem for the chapel of the

Other treasures of the Cathedral include the Chapter and Columbian Library, with 90,000 volumes, dating from the donations of Alfonso X and including the Book of Hours belonging to Queen Isabella the Catholic and the 20,000 volumes donated by Fernando Colón (the son of Christopher Columbus) with texts and documents of his father.

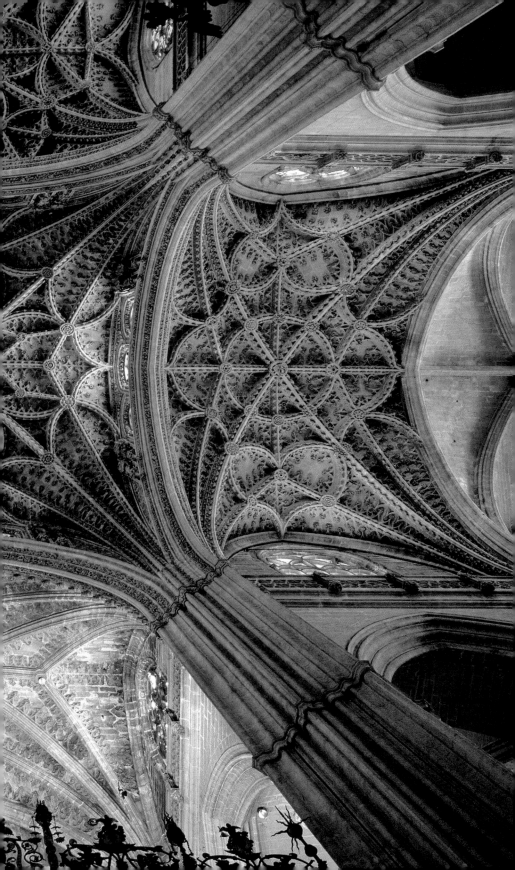

On these pages, the Sacristía Mayor and the Alfonsine tables.

The Cathedral of Seville

The building and its contents may be considered as an anthology of the many styles and works of art produced over the centuries it took to construct. It was started in the 15th century in late Gothic style on the foundations of the old mosque, of which important parts remain such as the Patio de los Naranjos and above all, the Giralda. The Sacristía Mayor and the Capilla Real date from the 16th century. From this renaissance style evolved the exuberant baroque of other parts of the building. The Cathedral contains a collection of paintings and sculptures dating from the 15th century that is of world importance.

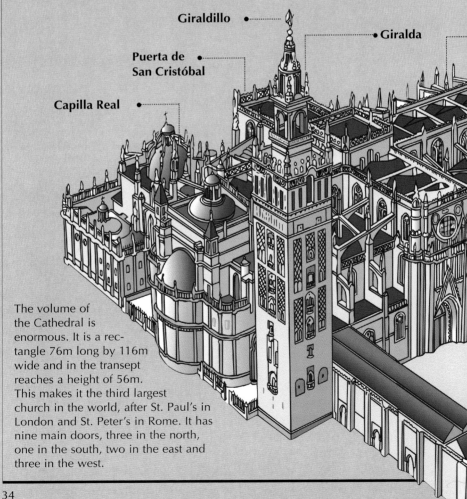

Giraldillo

Giralda

Puerta de
San Cristóbal

Capilla Real

The volume of the Cathedral is enormous. It is a rectangle 76m long by 116m wide and in the transept reaches a height of 56m. This makes it the third largest church in the world, after St. Paul's in London and St. Peter's in Rome. It has nine main doors, three in the north, one in the south, two in the east and three in the west.

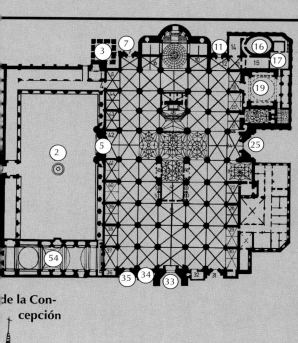

de la Con-
cepción

Patio de los
Naranjos

Puerta del
Perdón

KEY TO PLAN

1.-Puerta del Perdón
2.-Patio de los Naranjos
3.-Giralda
4.-Puerta del Lagarto
5.- Puerta de la Concepción
6.-Capilla del Pilar
7.-Puerta de los Palos
8.-Capilla de San Pedro
9.-Capilla Real
10.-Capilla de la Concepción Grande
11.-Puerta de las Campanillas
12.-Altar de las Santas Justa y Rufina
13.-Capilla del Mariscal
14.-Sala de ornamentos
15.- Antecabildo
16.- Sala Capitular
17.- Patio del Mariscal
18.-Transito a la sacristía Mayor
19.- SACRISTÍA Mayor
20.- Capilla de San Andrés
21.- Capilla los Dolores
22.-SACRISTÍA de los Cálices
23.- Patio de los Óleos
24.- Monumento a Colón
25.- Puerta de San Cristóbal
26.- Capilla de la Antigua
27.- Capilla de Hermenegildo
28.-Capilla de San José
29.- Capilla de San Ana
30.- Capilla de San Laureano
31.- Puerta de San Miguel
32.-Capilla de San Isidoro
33.- Puerta de la Asunción
34.- Capilla de San Leandro
35.- Puerta del Bautismo
36.- Capilla de los Jacomes
37.- Portada del Sagrario
38.- Capilla de San Antonio
39.- Capilla de Scalas
40.- Capilla de Santiago
41.- Capilla de San Francisco
42.- Crucero Brazo Norte
43.- Capilla de las doncellas
44.- Capilla de los evangelistas
45.- Capilla Mayor
46.-Crucero
47.- Coro
48.- Pórtico del coro
49.- Capilla de la Concepción chica
50.-Capilla de la Encarnación
51.-Encarnación
52.-Capilla de La Estrella
53.- Capilla de San Gregorio
54.- Iglesia del Sagrario

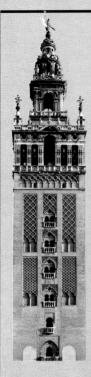

•THE GIRALDA
The original Muslim minaret was 70m high, but with the Christian addition it is now nearer 94m. It is said that the Castillian king Fernando III, the Saint, climbed to the top on horseback the day the city was taken: there is no staircase but instead a gently sloping ramp which rises up to just below the belfry. The climb is well worth the visit for the superb views.

The Giralda

The Giralda is the most graceful and slender of the three surviving Almohad minarets; the others are the Kutubiyya in Marrakesh and the Hasan Tower, Rabat. It is also one of the very few buildings of Islamic Spain left unscathed by Christian intervention as it was taken over practically untouched, although given new symbolism, as the Cathedral bell tower. The minaret was started in 1184 by the architect Ibn Basso with a base of stone blocks, some of which are Roman. After a pause of four years, work restarted under Ali al-Gomari, this time in brick, and ten years later he finished it off with the 'yamur' or pinnacle with four great spheres.

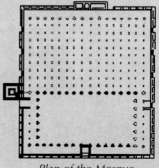

Plan of the Mosque

The central body of the tower is made up of chambers one on top of the other with Almohad vaulting, and around which climbs the ramp which

lessens in width and incline as it rises. The 1356 earthquake, which damaged the Alcázar (constructed during the reign of Pedro I), also brought down the yamur (pinnacle of the Mosque), replaced in 1400 by a bell-tower. In 1558 Hernán Ruiz the Younger, at the height of the Renaissance and during construction of the cathedral, was inspired to create the five separate, ascending bodies that make up the addition. The first, and largest, is known as Campanas (the bells), followed by Reloj (the clock), Estrellas (the stars), Redondo (the round) and,

highest of all, Penacho (the crest). Topping it, as did the yamur (pinnacle) before it, is the Giraldillo, the winged statue above the Giralda tower, symbolising the triumph of the Christian faith.

Original construction   First alteration   Today

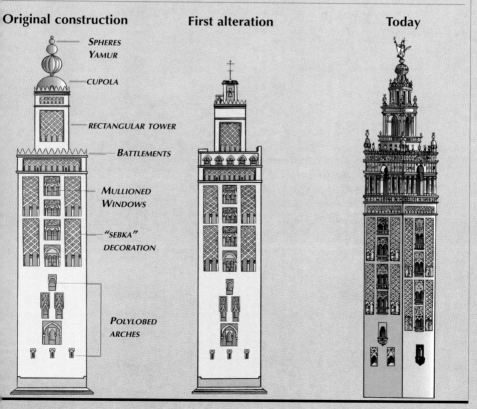

- SPHERES
- YAMUR
- CUPOLA
- RECTANGULAR TOWER
- BATTLEMENTS
- MULLIONED WINDOWS
- "SEBKA" DECORATION
- POLYLOBED ARCHES

•FAÇADE OF THE PALACIO DE DON PEDRO. *This palace, of Abbadid origin, was built for king Don Pedro by craftsmen from Granada and Toledo accustomed to adapting the remains of old Almohad palaces to the new taste for the Mudéjar style. This style uses designs, decorations and techniques of Muslim origin and taste to incorporate them in Christian buildings; wood used as a decorative element, shaped bricks laid out in rhomboid patterns (Sebka), polylobed*

arches, calligraphic arabic inscriptions and so on. Granadine architects copied this façade in the Mexuar of the Alhambra (see above).

•ENGRAVING OF THE REALES ALCÁ-   ZARES

The Reales Alcázares

This palace complex dates back to the tenth century Caliphal palace-fortress. It has been adapted and remodelled according to the necessities and taste of each reigning mornarch up to the present time.

Archaeological excavations have revealed that in Roman times there existed an important commercial and military settlement on the banks of the River Guadalquivir. It was from the eleventh century, however, with the Moorish taifa kingdoms, during the Abbadid dynasty, that the area became the centre of an influential state, following the Caliphate tradition.

Successful invasions by the Almoravids in 1086 and, especially, by the Almohads in 1146, introduced features that today are typical of Seville, the pools, arches and patios containing fountains, trees and flowers.

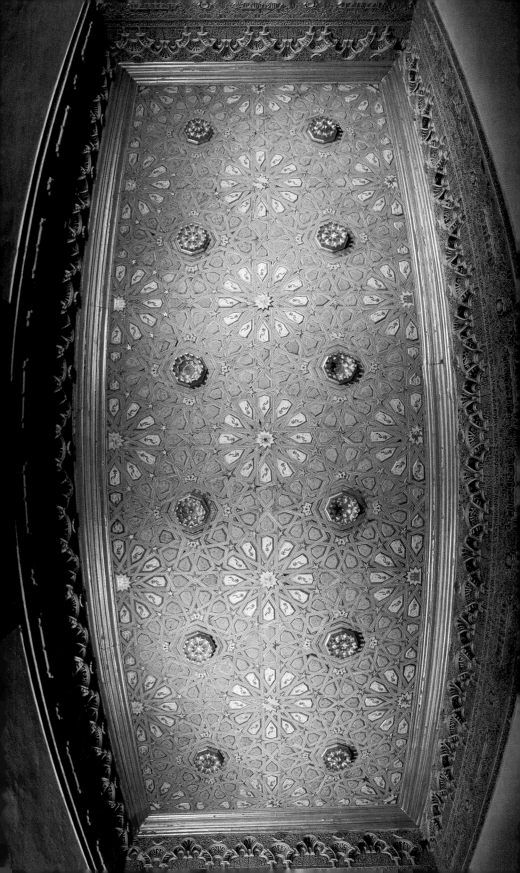

• THE PATIO DE LAS DONCELLAS
As can be seen by the proportions and decoration, this

patio (of the Dolls), was the centre of court life in the palace. The ground floor (14th c.), is in the mudéjar style with poly-lobed arches, columns in pairs and the original dado. Above it is 16th century arcaded gallery with balustrades, which harmonises perfect-ly with the very dif-ferent architectural style below.
On these pages are several views of the patio.

This Almohad style spread like sweet perfume through-out the Moorish lands of Al-Andalus as far as the Alham-bra palace in Granada, where it is still admired, cen-turies later.

After Seville was taken in 1248 by Ferdinand III, his son, Alfonso X the Wise, had a Gothic palace constructed, and it was during this period, and in Seville and Toledo, that the exclusively Spanish art form known as Mudéjar was forged. This was a syn-thesis of the two cultures, in which Almohad decorative styles were incorporated, seamlessly, into Gothic Christian art. The summit of understanding between the two cultures was attained during the reign of Pedro I

('the Cruel') of Castille, who placed personal and political relationships above religious beliefs. Ten years after the

earthquake of 1356, he had the Alcázares reconstructed as a royal palace; it was sub-

•PATIO DE LAS MUÑECAS *(150º view). A small intimate patio with a delicate air and rich decoration of Nasrid influence. The upper floors (right) are a 19th century restoration.*

• 19TH CENTURY ENGRAVING OF A MOORISH PATIO

sequently adapted to the tastes and necessities of his successors. The Renaissance style was adopted during the reign of Charles V, whose influence is particularly evident in the Patio de las Muñecas (above), with its columns, coats of arms and other decorative elements.

The Salón de Embajadores (Ambassadors Hall), together with the neighbouring Patio de las Doncellas, formed the heart of the complex, around which were the royal chambers. The structure of the hall, in its dimensions and arrangement, copies that of the former Abbadid palace, with triple caliphate arches whose splendour was inspired by those of Medina Zahara near Cordoba. The decoration, however, from its more elaborately worked ornamentation and the brilliance of its colours, is typical of the Mudejar innovations of King Pedro I, with an evident

Nasrid influence. There are innumerable highly worked capitals, booty brought from

the palatine city of Cordoba by al-Mutamid, then resident in the palace, for his beloved Rumainkiya, as Abderramán III had done before him. King Pedro I, moreover, probably had the palace remodelled for his lover María de Padilla. The Patio de las Muñecas also lies within the heart of the palace chambers, but is somewhat set apart and has a more intimate atmosphere. Its elegant proportions have retained their charm despite innovations such as the added height. The columns, of varying colour and hue seem hardly capable of bearing the capitals above, adding to the overall impression of fragility. The rhom-

boidal decoration, in stucco and dating from Almohad times, contributes still more to the airs of transparency and grace. The wooden fretwork over the doorways and covering the ceilings is an

●**ENGRAVINGS OF THE REALES ALCÁZARES** *The Patio de las Muñecas, left. Hall of the Ambassadors in the centre and a romantic composition above.*

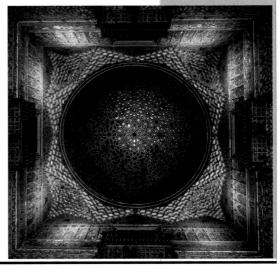

• **HALL OF THE AMBAS-SADORS.** (*above and previous pages*).

• **TAPESTRY-MAP OF CHARLES V'S** *Tunisian war. Spain appears as viewed from cental Europe, that is, 'upside down'. (Right).*

• **WOODEN CEILINGS** (*Opposite*) *in the palace, most dating from the times of the Catholic Monarchs.*

outstanding feature of the Alcázares. This work carried out by Moorish carpenters, also seen in Castilian churches and palaces, was readily adaptable to different uses and ideologies, as the designs were pre-dominantly geometric. This aspect was of crucial importance to Islam and posed no conflict with the Christian faith; furthermore, it was capable of almost unlimited development in terms of its composition and aes-thetics. The gar-dens, in which each epoch and culture left their mark, form an important part of the complex. Indeed, the gardens and the buildings around them were always consid-ered to be interrelated and created with this in mind.

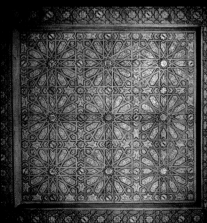

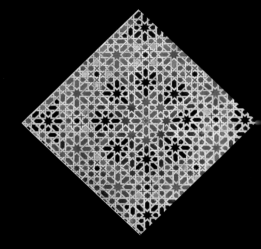

<u>Los Reales Alcázares</u> (The Royal fortress)

One of the most remarkable things about the Reales Alcázares is that , reflecting the history of the city, building and alteration work took over ten centuries and so the buildings comprise the essence of each moment of that history lived and of each artistic influence, native or foreign, worthy enough to leave its mark.Over the centuries Seville has been like a perfect matron, stern yet kind, quickly dominating those who came to dominate, and the cradling arms that within a remarkably short time the impetuous conquerers would seek out. The Alcázares buildings are thus a synthesis of the creative arts from the Caliphate to the renaissance.

●**GEOMETRICAL DESIGN**

In Islamic art, a repetitive rhythm, above all in geometry, is one of many ways to express the unity of Allah. Mosaic decoration is an especially suitable medium for this iteration.

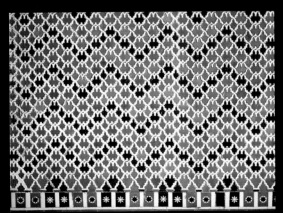

• Almost all of these mosaics were made by Muslim craftsmen working for Christians, and although some were brought here from the Alhambra in the 16th C., we should not forget that there was an important cultural and commercial interchange between Granada and Seville in the 14th C. The demand for Granadine potters was especially great; many set up their workshops in the Triana district and some of these are still there.

•GARDENS OF THE REALES ALCÁZARES Although they have suffered, as have the palace biuldings, changes over the centuries the gardens are still impressive for their size and variety of styles from Mannerist corners to Romantic arbours.

▶CHARLES V PAVILION AND VIEW OF THE GARDENS. THE WEDDING OF CHARLES V to the princess Isabel of Portugal in 1526 in the rich city of Seville clearly demonstrated the interest (in more senses than one) of the emperor in the city. For this event he remodelled the Alcázar and ordered his pavilion from Juan Hernández, with mudéjar and Renaissance elements.

➤ This 16th century tiling in the Patio de las Doncellas is a good example of the evolution of ceramic mosaics which for centuries filled the dados of Sevillian houses.

SEVILLE

in focus

Walk through the Santa Cruz district
Casa de Pilatos

Left, cupola of the Hall of the Ambassadors (Reales Alcázares)

The Santa Cruz Quarter

Although it was reconstructed in the early twentieth century, this quarter still expresses the very essence of Seville. It is also known as the Jewish quarter, as it was here, around the Alcázar, where Ferdinand III and Alfonso X accommodated the Jews after their expulsion by the Moors. The Jews were well treated by Pedro I during the 14th century, but suffered severe persecution

1391 and were finally expelled a century later, when their synagogues, previously mosques, were turned into Christian churches. The quarter, which retains its secular structure, reflects the urban development of Seville, both in its Moorish and in its Christian periods. The Moors ignored the rigid geometry of Roman

architecture and their white-washed houses crowded together around the mosques, their daily meeting places, in a labyrinth of streets and blind alleys. These were very narrow, to provide protection against the harsh summer sun, while the houses were constructed around patios containing a fountain or well and with abundant vegetation. The Christian reconquest brought the introduction of squares, parishes and public open spaces. The Santa Cruz quarter is a mixture of these elements: the patio, previously a private space, is now open

to view, but discreetly, through barred windows and doorways. A fresh surprise awaits the visitor around every corner.

Hospital de los Venerables
This former shelter for destitute priests was built in the late 17th century in a Baroque style with a simple patio based on linear forms and an exuberant chapel that is one of the finest examples of Andalusian Baroque, containing paintings by Valdés Leal. The painter Murillo also worked for this foundation, and his House-

Museum is nearby. Today it is the headquarters of the Focus Foundation.

Another memorable area is that formed by the Callejón del Agua and Calle de la Pimienta, while the most well known of all is the Plaza de Doña Elvira, lined with orange trees, near the former Corral de Comedias, where music in the open air is often to be heard. The white and yellow-painted houses contrast with the vivid colours of the ceramics in the workshops that are characteristic of the Triana district of Seville. Also worth seeing are the Plaza de Alfaro, the setting for the

•Plaza de la Santa Cruz *This might be taken as the most typically Sevillian of the city's plazas. It is characterized by such Andalusian craftsmanship as the wrought-iron of the balcony grilles and the little lanterns hanging from the Cruz de la Cerrajería, the cross crowning the square, which is a masterpiece of 17th century baroque ironwork. The painter Murillo was buried here.*

•Don Juan
The famous fictional Sevillian character was invented by Tirso de Molina, although he may have been based on Don Miguel Maraña, founder of the Hospital de la Caridad. Later authors and composers inspired by him include Molière, Mozart, Dumas, Byron and José Zorilla. There is a statue of him in the Plaza de Refinadores.

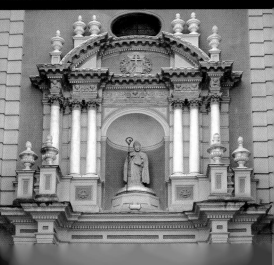

- **FAÇADE OF THE CASA DE PILATOS.** *This sumptuous palace complex was built by D. Fadrique Enríquez de Ribera on his return from a pilgrimage to Jerusalem in 1519. The façade, with its classicist triumphal arch, is reminiscent of Roman villas.*

- **CENTRAL PATIO OF THE PALACE.** *With a mixture of decorative elements, Renaissance forms and classical sculptures. (Right) An engraving of the patio.*

opera "The Marriage of Figaro", and the Plaza de la Santa Cruz, with its magnificent seventeenth-century wrought-iron cross at the centre. In the Plaza de los Refinadores stands the statue of the proud figure of Don Juan, a native of Seville who is familiar world-wide and who inspired Molière and Mozart, among others. The heart of the Jewish quarter was San Bartolomé quarter, where colourful houses lined streets such as Leviés.

■ LA CASA DE PILATOS

The Renaissance arrived in Spain in the early sixteenth century, imported by enlightened noblemen such as the Tendillas and the Mendozas, who were to have such an influence on contemporary architecture. In Seville, it was Fadrique Enríquez, the Marquess of Tarifa, who, dazzled by the splendour of Italian classicism, commissioned the construction of this palace, which was the

inspiration and guide for so many other distinguished houses in the city after 1533. The front of the building,

with its classical arches, is reminiscent of a Roman villa. The name of the palace refers to the house of Pontios Pilate in Jerusalem, where its owner had been on a pilgrimage, which would be the inspiration

for the Holy Week proces-
sions in Seville.

The central patio is pure

Italian classicism: two large
sculptures, the Greek god-
desses Ceres and Minerva,
(Athena) preside the corners,
there are busts of emperors
along the walls, and in the
centre is a Genovese marble
fountain beneath a statue of
Janus, the Roman god with
two faces, gazing in opposite directions. The first floor
features a Gothic balustrade
and Renaissance arches,

while the Mudejar influence
is represented by socles and
stuccoed panelling and
arches above plain columns.
This juxtaposition and mix-
ing of styles, the harmonious
blending of elements and
materials, produces a won-

• THE CENTRAL PATIO

• **PLATERESQUE 16YH. CENTURY GRILLE.** *The Casa de Pilatos contains an extraordinary wealth of art treasures.*

derful sense of balance, the essence of what has come to be termed the Seville style. A further attraction, and quite as interesting as the palace itself and its surroundings, is the extraordinary archaeological collection displayed both in the patios known as El Grande and El Chico (the large one and the small one), in the two gardens and in the rooms and upstairs.

The descendents of the family, later intermarried with the

Medicis, completed this unique collection with works of classical art and the priceless private archive of the ducal family

• **VIEWS OF ONE OF THE PATIOS.** *Below, statue of Minerva or Athena.*

SEVILLE

in focus

Places of interest
Ayuntamiento
La Torre del Oro
Museo de Bellas Artes
Hospital de la Caridad
The Maestranza Bullring

Ayuntamiento

The History of the Town Hall is linked to the wedding of Charles V to his cousin Isabel in 1526. At that time the town council decided to move into the Lonja or mercantile exchange in the Plaza San Francisco and construct a new building worthy of the event and of a city which, after the discovery of America in 1492, was being remodelled as the financial capital of the empire. Diego de Riaño, who had already worked on the Cathedral, directed the work for seven years in which he built the south and east façades in the purest Renaissance style.

In the Chapter House upstairs are housed the municipal archives, which contain a wealth of important documents on the history of Seville dating from the time of the Catholic Monarchs. The Council also owns an important collection of paintings derived from the 19th C. desentailments of religious houses, and including works by Velázquez, Zurbarán, Valdés Leal and Murillo.

•VIEW OF THE TOWN HALL
This engraving of 1738 shows a Corpus Christi prossession passing through the Plaza San Francisco. The Town Hall is in the background.(Below) The arms of Seville and the rebus of Alfonso X, 'no-made-ja-do' ('it has not abandoned me').

•THE EAST FAÇADE GIVING ON TO THE PLAZA SAN FRANCISCO.
This façade was built by Diego de Riaño in the first decades of the 16th century when the Renaissance, embellished with plateresque decoration, took firm root in Spain. The interesting medallions depict mythical and historical people, prominent among them Hercules and Caesar, legendary founders of the city.

As can be seen from the upper window on the right, the building was never finished and there were serious problems in finishing off the other façade on Plaza Nueva in the 19th century.

•THE MEDALLIONS *not only represent classical gods and heroes, wishfully connected to the history of Seville, but also details alluding to the recent wedding of Charles V which serve to affirm the grandeur of the historic moment.*

•THE TORRE DEL ORO. *This is really a bulwark tower, the final link in the extensive city wall joining the Alcázares and the strategically important dock.*

The Torre del Oro

This is Seville's other famous tower, situated on the banks of the Guadalquivir in the well-known Arenal district, and with la Giralda one of the symbols of the city.

The name Torre del Oro (Gold Tower) comes from the gold tiles which once covered it and not from the American gold bullion which, although it was unloaded hereabout, was in fact stored in the nearby Casa de la Moneda (mint). Today it houses a small maritime museum.

It was built between 1220 and 1221 by the governor Abul-Ula, and is one of the last Almo-had buildings of which Seville has such a rich cultural heritage. Phot.1868 by J. Laurent.

18th century engraving from Laborde's book depicting unloading at the dockside.

Torre del Oro, 13th century

- 18th century addition
- Battlements
- Central tower
- Blind horse-shoe arches
- Dodecagon construction

• *The Baroque façade contrasts with the Neoclassical building.*

Museo de Bellas Artes.

The Fine Arts Museum is housed in the former Convento de la Merced a Baroque building of the beginning of the 17th century, itself a remodelling of an older building. The Museum was created in 1835 to house works of art confiscated in that year with the desentailment of religious properties. The collection of Baroque paintings of the Seville school is outstanding and as a gallery it ranks second in the country. It also contains collections of ceramics and masterpieces of sculpture as well as decorative architectural pieces.

'*The Virgin of the Caves by Francisco de Zurbarán, 17th century. Sala V is the old church.*

There are three patios a grand cloister and a central staircase.
A collection of tiles from different convents is displayed in the vestibule.
Sala I contains Gothic paintings by Bartolomé Bermejo and the Renaissance Sala, Gerard David, Torrigiano (left), Alejo Fernández, Morales, Lucas Cranach, El Greco and more.

'Santiago El Mayor' by José de Ribera, 16th century.

Murillo, with the pictures he painted for the now disappeared Capuchin convent.

Sala VI on the second floor contains more Spanish and Seville school Baroque paintings with a 'St. Paul' by Ribera and work by Alonso Cano. Sala VII is dedicated to

El Greco's portrait of his son, Jorge Manuel.

Sala V, the old church, now houses a major collection of paintings of the Seville Baroque school. These include Roelas with his 'Martyrdom of St. Andrew', Zurbarán with 'The Apotheosis of St. Thomas', and canvases by Herrera the Elder and, above all,

«La Dolorosa». by Murillo, 17th century.

Murillo and his followers; Sala VIII to Valdés Leal and Sala X to Zurbarán with 17 canvases, including the famous ones painted for the Seville Carthusian monastery, where Martínez Montañes also worked. Sala XII contains the Sevillian school and XIII the Romantics.

'Portrait of Don Cristóbal Súarez' de Ribera by Diego Velazquez (1620).

'El Canónigo Duaro' by Francisco de Goya.

Iglesia de San Luis

● **INTERIOR PATIO**
This is a double patio each part with a central fountain containing motifs alluding to compassion and charity and surrounded and connected by galleries of Tuscan arches.

On the walls are panels of Dutch tiles.

El Hospital de la Caridad

Although this Charity Hospital has existed since the 15th century, it was refounded in 1674 by Miguel de Mañara and his Charity Brotherhood. They built the Baroque church which has only one nave and decorated it with edifying pictures and sculptures exemplifying the religious virtues, above all charity, the raison d'être of the order. The artists chosen include Valdés Leal, who painted, 'In ictu oculi' (in the blink of an eye) and 'Finis gloriae mundi' (thus ends the glory of the world), two canvases allusive to vanity, death and bodily decomposition. Another was Murillo, who painted eleven masterpieces on more agreeable subjects. There are only seven here now as the French Marshal Soult pillaged four of them in 1810, and include 'St. John of God with the sick' and 'St. Elizabeth of Hungary and the boy with ringworm'.

Among the greatest masterpieces of Baroque sculpture is Pedro Roldán's tableau of the Entombment (right), set in

an altarpiece of gilt and black by Valdés Leal. This retable (left), has all the typical devices of Baroque art and can be taken as characteristic of many others in Seville; a base with Salomonic columns on either side supporting the entablature, and based on a play of extruding and intruding volumes, wavy lines, complicated rhythms and twisting

movements and all with the purpose of exulting the tableau within.

The façade also has a retable structure (above), with 18th century tiling. There are two Baroque patios in the building designed by Falconete, with polygonal fountain basins in the middle and Italianate figures alluding once again to charity.

• **ELEVATION OF THE FAÇADE.** *This was finished by Leonardo de Figueroa and is one of the clearest examples of a façade in retable form, not only for the structure in floors, but also for the subject matter depicted in tiles; St. George, Santagio, Faith, Hope and Charity.*

• **THE ENTOMBMENT** *by Pedro Roldan*

• **PRINCIPAL FAÇADE OF THE REAL MAESTRANZA.** *(Above) The Prince´s box, dating from the beginning of the 19th century.*

• **ENGRAVING OF THE BULLRING.** *Below. 19th century drawing of the façade by Richard Ford.*

Bullring of la Maestranza

Another monument emblematic of Sevilla is the Real Maestranza de Caballería (Royal Equestrian Society), which dates back to the 18th century. The old tradition of bullfighting on horseback at popular fiestas was supported by the Society, on which Philip V, the first Bourbon king, conferred the title 'Royal'. In 1707 building began, in the Arenal district, a popular recreation area, on a bullring (but square) made of wood, which was progressively restored and altered, until by 1761 part of it, still to be seen, was finished to the plans of Vicente San Martín, but now in stone. Twenty years later the wonderful Prince's box was finished, and named in

honour of the king's son. It was designed by the Portuguese Cayetano de Acosta. The bullring seen today was

not completely finished until 1881. Inside is a museum with exhibits ranging in date from the beginning of bullfighting to the present day.

Among them are bronzes by Benlliure and a drawing by Picasso.

SEVILLE
in focus

A stroll to the Parque de María Luisa
Palacio de San Telmo
Fabrica de Tabaco
Parque de María Luisa
The Spanish-American Exhibition of 1929
Plaza de España
Plaza de América

Previous double- page, Patio of the Condesa de Lebrija palace.
Left, palace of San Telmo.

• **THE PRINCIPAL FAÇADE OF THE PALACIO DE SAN TELMO.** *Formerly the seat of the Marine University; it now houses the Andalusian Regional Government.*

• **DETAIL OF THE FAÇADE OF THE PALACE BY FIGUEROA.**

A stroll to the Parque de María Luisa

At the end of the 19th century and starting at the Puerta de Jerez the historic heart of Sevilla underwent important urban reforms. Part of the garden of the Palace of San Telmo became the María Liusa Park and in the neighbourhood of the old Tobacco factory the Hotel Alfonso XIII was built.

■ **PALACIO DE SAN TELMO**
This attractive baroque-style building, now the seat of the Andalusian Regional Government, was opened in 1682 as a College-Seminary for naval orphans, by the Marine University.
This explains its name, as San Telmo is the patron saint of sailors. It became a College of Nautical Studies in 1788, for the training of pilots and master navigators. Subsequently it became the property of the Duke and Duchess of Montpensier, who made it their residence in 1848 , when the palace was one of the landmarks of romantic Seville.

Princess María Luisa, in her will, left it to the Archbishopric of Seville and it was converted into a Diocesan Seminary in 1901. In addition to the facade, by Figueroa, noteworthy fea-

tures include the staircase and the Columned Salon.

■ **FABRICA DE TABACO.**
Today the administrative centre of Seville University, this was one of the largest and most well-known buildings in Spain during the 18th century, and among the most innovative in pre-industrial Europe. The former tobacco factory was, in its day, considered a revolutionary structure, due to innovations such as its modular layout, the underground channelling system to maintain internal humidity, and a complex system of ventilation.

The production of tobacco was a lucrative state monopoly in which up to 3000 women were employed.

■ **HOTEL ALFONSO XII.**
This luxurious building, in Neo-Mudejar style, was built during the 1920s for the Spanish-American Exhibition of 1929. It is considered

to be representative of the regionalist style, and inspired by historical criteria. The Exhibition Casino and the Lope de Vega Municipal Theatre, which comprised the Seville Pavilion in the Exhibition, are nearby.

•**FAÇADE OF THE OLD TOBACCO FACTORY**, *now headquarter of the university.*

• *(Above) 19th century photograph by J. Laurent of the palace of San Telmo. (Left) Alameda de Hercules*

•**COAT OF ARMS OF THE TOBACCO FACTORY.**

• KEY TO PLAN.
(PARQUE DE MARÍA LUISA)

1.-Plaza de España
2.-Museo arqueológico.
3.-Museo de arte y costumbres populares.
4.-Pabellón Real.
5.-Glorieta de Cervantes.
6.-Glorieta de los hermanos Machado.
7.-Glorieta de los Quintero.
8.-Fuente de los Leones.
9.- Estanque de los patos.
10.- Glorieta Azul.
11.- Estanque de los lotos.
12.- Glorieta de Becquer.
13.- Glorieta de Portugal.
14.- Pabellón de USA.
15.- Monumento a Elcano.
16.- Pabellón de Argentina.
17.- Pabellón de Brasil.
18.- Pabellón de México.
19.- Pabellón de Colombia.
20.- Pabellón de Marruecos.
21.- Monumento a Simón Bolivar.
22.- Jardines de las Delicias.

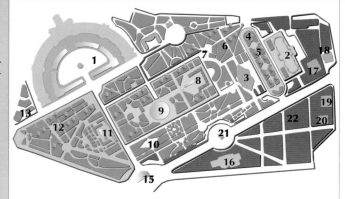

• MONUMENT TO BECQUER.

The Sevillian Gustavio Adolfo Becquer (1836-1870), was considered the poet par excellence of romantic Spanish Literature. Among his works are, 'Rimas', 'Leyendas' and 'Cartas...'.

■ PARQUE DE MARÍA LUISA

To a large degree, the charm of Seville is due to its welcoming parks and gardens in the heart of the city; these lend a delicate perfume to the city streets, particularly in the spring. The Alcázar and the Murillo gardens were generously enlarged by Princess María Luisa in 1893, when she donated half of her own gardens from the San Telmo Palace. This much-needed new space in the city thus became the park that today bears her name. In correspondence with the times in which they were created, these gardens, designed by the Fren-chman Forestier, are romantic, bucolic and inspire nostalgia. Today, of course, they also provide a beneficial green space in the centre of a city that is becoming more and more hectic and cosmopolitan. The gardens

were inaugurated in 1914, and special attention was paid to the plants and flowers, to the ever-present water in pools, fountains and springs, and to the many monuments dedicated to illustrious names from the past, both from Seville and elsewhere: Gustavo Adolfo Becquer, the Álvarez

• THE PARK
Antique and modern views of the Parque de María Luisa which, although it is still not a hundred years old is already a fundamental part of the city and indespensible lung for its inhabitants.

Quintero brothers, and Antonio and Manuel Machado. Also represented are historical characters such as Dante and Cervantes, and famous contemporary literary figures. The park is also an important botanical garden, with a considerable wealth and diversity of species; it extends over 38 hectares and contains around 1000 palm trees and more than 3000 trees of other species. Seville, in competition with Bilbao, won the right to host the 1929 Spanish-American Exhibition. The new space provided by the María Luisa Park was an ideal site for the various pavilions, which provided a new outlook on the area and signified a substantial change to the city, revolutionising its conception of urban living and character.

91

ded on a new concept for a colonnaded public space in which the emphasis would be on its welcoming nature and agreeable environment; that is to say, a place to relax in rather than the busy commercial squares of old. This concept, so up-to-date, is now a requisite for any urban development.

The Spanish-American Exhibition of 1929

The original idea for the Exhibition arose from the possibility of hosting a cultural event of international scope, at a time when commercial fairs were in decline, and as an attractive way of encouraging tourism. With this in mind, the architect Aníbal González designed a series of buildings and pavilions to be constructed within the María Luisa Park, thus creating the monumental twin spaces of the Plaza de España and the Plaza de América, surrounded by lush vegetation. These developments came to be landmarks within the revitalised city of Seville.

■ **The Plaza de España.**
This Plaza is in the north western area of the Park, beside the Plaza de América. It is semi-circular in shape, 170 metres in diameter and 100 metres wide. It boasts a porticoed gallery and is flanked by two 80-metre-high towers. Bordering the Plaza is a canal crossed by Venetian-style footbridges that are adorned with balustrades of ceramics from the popular Seville quarter

known as Triana. At the base of the semi-circle there are benches decorated with painted tiled panels, one for each province in Spain, illustrating historical episodes. This Plaza was the focal point of the

Exhibition, and was conceived to evoke a Palladian-style villa. The combination of brickwork, ceramics and carpentry offered new

• **PLAZA DE ESPAÑA.**
The cut and carved brickwork was also used for the figures, but accompanied by ceramic designs in bright colours which break the monotony of the brick colour.
On the following page, details of the ceramic work on the benches.

creative possibilities, and reinterpreted the forms and volumes of Mudejar art by which it was inspired.

Marble was used as a complementary material, to vary the rhythm and to highlight differences in textures, while stone was also incorporated when the architect wished to suggest Renaissance art.

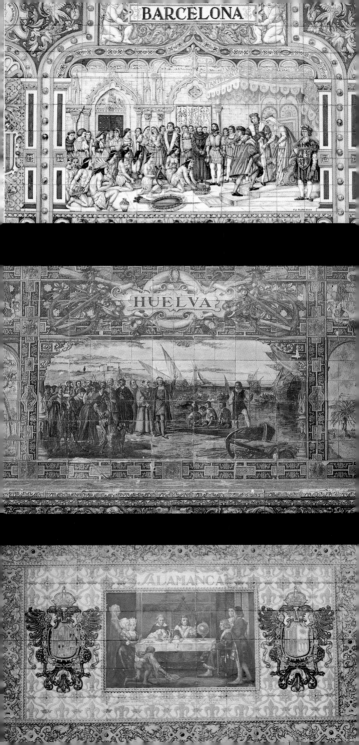

• **THE MUSEO ARQUE-OLÓGICO** *was founded in 1946 in the Neo-Renaissance pavilion of the Spanish American Exhibition. It contains an extensive collection of objects from different ages and cultures of the Guadalquivir valley, from the palaeolithic to the 16th C. It also houses the famous Carambolo treasure hoard of gold jewellery dating from 650 BC., testimony of the importance and cultural advancement of Itálica, above all under Trajan and Hadrian. Visigothic and caliphal artefacts occupy the last rooms.*

■ Plaza de América.

In the southern part of the María Luisa Park and facing the Plaza de España, this too was designed by Aníbal González, as the Exhibition's principal Space of Honour. To achieve this goal, it was intended to form a synthesis of styles from the history of Seville architecture; from Mudejar to Neo-Classicism, Gothic-Plateresque to Renaissance and Baroque. This wealth of styles resulted in a new tendency known as historicist art or traditional regionalism. The Plaza is oriented around three pavilions: the Mudéjar, the Real and the Pabellón del Renacimiento which today houses the Archaeological Museum.

THE PABELLÓN REAL: Built of bricks and glazed ceramics, in the late-Gothic style

known as Isabelline, a style that was employed in countless churches and monasteries during the 14th and 15th centuries.

THE PABELLÓN MUDÉJAR:

Taking its inspiration from mediaeval Islamic aesthetics, this pavilion forms a

•MUSEO DE COSTUMBRES POPULARES

This Popular Arts & Customs Museum was formerly the Mudéjar pavilion and from 1972 the Ethnographic Museum. It has rooms for temporary exhibitions. Although some are older, most of the exhibits date from the 19th and 20th centuries, with a great variety of traditional costumes, utensils and tools of all sorts, agricultural implements, jewels, lamps, silver-, glass- and woodwork, as well as works of popular craftsmanship. There is also a good collection of the local Triana ceramic ware.

pleasing synthesis of Caliphate, Nasrid and Mudejar influences.

At present it contains the Museum of Popular Arts and Customs.

THE RENAISSANCE PAVILION: Today, this pavilion houses the Archaeological and Fine Arts Museums.

Following pages: the Costurero de la Reina building, a window in the pabellón de Perú and the pabellón del Renacimiento.

• **DIFFERENT PAVILIONS (ABOVE, PERU).**
They are concentrated in the Parque María Luisa and those that survive are; Argentina, Brazil, Colombia, Cuba, Chile, Dominican Republic, Guatemala, Morocco, Mexico, Peru, Portugal and Uruguay.

(Below) South American indians in the Colombia pavilion.

The first international exhibition of the twentieth century boasted over 100 pavilions and about 160,000 sq. metres dedicated to countries of, or influenced by, the Spanish-American world. The thirteen pavilions still remaining provide a good example of referential architecture, of a cultural expression of unity between peoples, a quality that has lasted to this day.

These pages show details of some pavilions: Mexico (above), with the colonial airs suggested by the Andalusian-style grille (left), and Portugal (opposite page), with undulating oriental roofs and the rotundate geometry of Peruvian inspiration, among others.

Opposite, the monuments to the Cid, the explorer Elcano and Theatre of Lope de Vega.

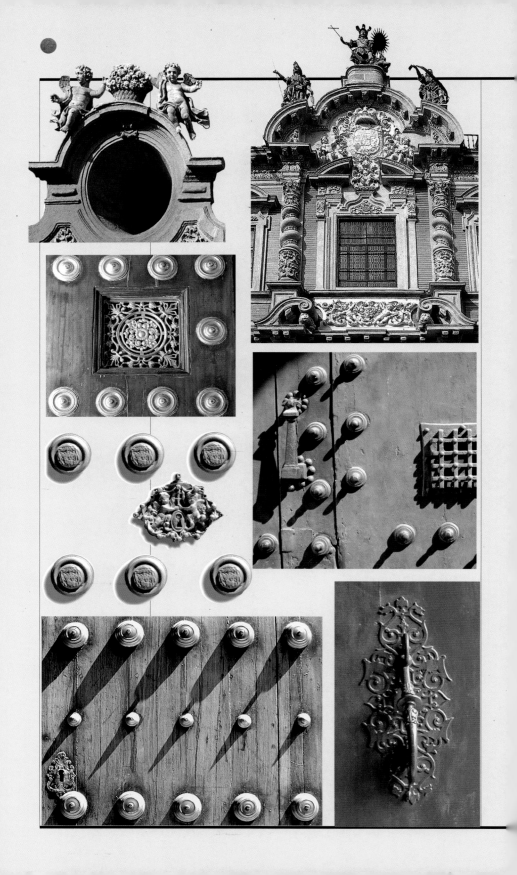

SEVILLE

in focus

Fiestas & popular traditions
Holy Week
The April fair

1970 Sra. VIRGEN GUADALUPE 1983

ANO 1967 NTRA. SRA. DEL MAR QUE SE VENERA EN ESTA IGLESIA 1967

BODEGA MATEO
FUNDADA EN 1938
Especialidad
en lomos de bacalao

SEMANA SANTA (HOLY WEEK) IN SEVILLE.
This is the high-point of the year in the city and the Sevillians work for months without rest decorating the heavy floats. These are borne by porters who might have to shoulder up to 50kg each for between four to twelve hours.

The colourful and attractive processions represent hours of annoy-mous effort and organisation, thus respecting the penitential spirituality that is the real reason behind the show which might, to some, seem merely folkloric.

Fiestas and Popular Traditions.

By long-established tradition, Seville's greatest festivals have been held in spring, and in almost uninterrupted fashion, as if wishing to celebrate every moment of the season. Thus, Holy Week is followed by the April Fair and then by the pilgrimage to the Virgin del Rocío. Although the latter is not exclusive to Seville, it is a heartfelt event and one of immense popularity in the city. After this, there is the May Crosses Festival and then Corpus Christi in June.

Semana Santa.

Although the Holy Week celebrations in Seville and elsewhere have been related to former pagan rites of spring, the true origin of this popular phenomenon, this public manifestation of the Christian faith, is more recent. In fact, it dates from the Council of Trent, when the Church favoured the explicit demonstration of religious feeling, the exaltation of the Eucharist and the dramatised spiritual instruction implicit in the processions. In the sixteenth century, Fadrique de Ribera, re-

enacted the Via Crucis he had witnessed on his pilgrimage to Jerusalem. The processions became firmly established during the seventeenth century, when associations of artisans and professionals decided to create Brotherhoods to bear the images with which they identified. There were more than 50 brotherhoods which, during Holy Week, participate in over 100 processions, following an established itinerary. The popularity of Holy

•IMAGES OF SEMANA SANTA. *An embroidered gown (above). (Above,left) The Expiration of Christ. (Left) One of the Holy Week floats, an below, exit from the church of the 'cachorro' (puppy) float.*

The exits of the pasos (floats) from their respective parish churches and later return, are the highlights of the processions. The officers directing the floats act with military precision and need all their expertise to guide the bearers, who, being underneath, are of course, moving 'blind'. Holy Week in Seville is replete with the scents of incense, orange blossom and of melting wax candles: of 'saetas', those spontaneous and anguished solos sung along the route, and of magical spring nights, all a little difficult to reconcile with the idea of suffering.

Week in Seville, internationally-renowned for hundreds of years for its spectacularity and colour, is in stark contrast to the Brotherhoods of Penitents. These pass by in silence, and their sobriety and sacrifice, their depth of religious feeling, overwhelm the festive mood. To the present day, this week is the most important of all the year in Seville.

•La Feria

The fair enclosure is entered through a monumental gate of different design each year. More than 1000 casetas are set up inside with streets, just like a small town and the lights and garlands fill the esplanade of the de los Remedios neighbourhood with life and colour.

The April Fair

Although the April Fair was founded in the mid-nineteenth century, its roots lie in the Middle Ages, when cattle fairs, commonplace in southern Andalusia, required an

annual meeting place at which animals could be bought and sold. These commercial occasions were always accompanied by a

more light-hearted side, which eventually came to overshadow and displace the original activity.

This was the case of the April Fair in Seville which, in turn, has served as a model for so many others throughout Andalusia. By tradition, the April Fair is always held one

•Las casetas

The caseta is a kind of home from home, some are private and others set up by associations, with eating and drinking facilities where the Sevillians can enjoy themselves together during one gay week in spring.

or two weeks after Easter Sunday. During recent times the Fair has undergone a

•THE FERIA AT THE BEGINNING OF THE 20TH CENTURY
These pictures show the origin of the Feria as a livestock fair, but even today there are horse parades and shows.

•FARALAES' COSTUME
This is also known as gypsy or flamenco dress and is from the Seville region, though its popularity has spread to other areas and to other fairs. Over time, it has been developed and adapted, but always provides spring in Seville with grace, colour and movement.

boom period, with more than 1000 'casetas', established in the fairground, known as Barrio de los Remedios. These are pavilions where people can eat, drink, chat and enjoy the music and dancing and which are a spectacle in themselves, being tremendously colourful, decorated with exquisite details and where the Seville people show off their finest costumes. The wide avenues of the fairground comprise a thoroughfare for wonderfully elegant Andalusian horses (and riders), sometimes harnessed to traditional carriages. The casetas are the rendezvous for reunions and parties that go on all week until the early hours of every morning.

SEVILLE

in focus

**A walk around the Cartuja Island
The Expo of 1992.**

The 'isla de la Cartuja' a flat space between two branches of the river Guadalquivir, was an ideal site for the universal exhibition of 1992, and eight new bridges were built to connect it with the city.

A walk around Cartuja Island

It is hoped that Sevilla's structural and technological development will be boosted in this strategic area completely changed by the Expo.

Although neither of the exhibitions held in Seville during the 20th century completely met the expectations for future development that had been placed on them, the city, in each case, received the benefits of modernisation and the improvement and transformation of the urban infrastructure.

After 1929, the former pavil-ions were turned into embassies, institutes, museums, cultural centres, etc., and after 1992, the 'intelligent' buildings constructed on Cartuja Island have been developed in two ways: on the one hand, there are private companies, now located within the new Science and

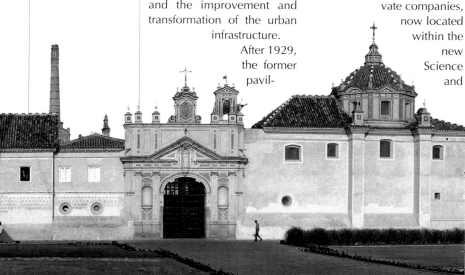

Technology Estate, where the University is also involved as part of its research programme On the other hand, there is a service sector focussed on the Isla Mágica (Magic Isle) Theme Park, which has recycled the buildings that were at the heart of the Expo '92 exhibition. The goal of this is to sat- isfy the increasing demand for multimedia and interactive events, incorporating state-of-the-art technology. One such application is the "Puerta Triana Cultural Space", which seeks to combine culture and entertainment; indeed, these have always been closely linked in Seville. Among the most

• **MONASTERIO DE SANTA MARÍA DE LAS CUEVAS.** *This was founded in 1400 although the church dates from the middle of the 15th century and was expanded in the 16th. The original monastic elements, Gothic, Mudéjar and Baroque, were restored as part of the Expo programme. For four centuries it has witnessed Sevillian life: Columbus stayed here when visiting and died and was buried here before his bones began their wanderings. It is now a museum, exhibitions centre and the headquarters of the Centro Andaluz de Arte Contemporáneo.*

• LA ISLA DE LA CARTU-JA *During the Expo this was the most important concentration of design and architecture of the* interesting results of the programme are the restoration of the Carthusian Monastery of Santa María de las Cuevas, the American garden, stocked with species from the Ame-ricas. Architectural innovations resulting from

end of th 20th century, marking new tendencies and aims for the future.

• EL PALENQUE *(Above) This was the grand theatre for the Expo and is now an exhibition centre of Andalusian music and culture.*

which had been a ceramics factory since it was confiscated from the Church in the 1830s. An interesting aspect that transcends the temporary nature of all such exhibitions was the creation of numerous open spaces, intended to create a localised mini-climate, in addition to the planting of botanical gardens such as

the Expo include spectacular and daringly-different new bridges over the River Gualdalquivir: the Fifth Centenary bridge, designed by José A. Fernán-dez and the emblematic Alamillo bridge by Santiago Calatrava, with a single suspension tower 138 metres high and 200 metres long.

SEVILLE

in focus

A tour through the province of Seville
Carmona
Écija
Osuna
Itálica

Left, a street in Carmona.

Carmona by D. Roberts

The province of Sevilla

The province of Seville has greatly vary-ing ecosystems and geographical fea-tures. The Sierra Morena rises in the north, with cork and holm-oak trees. This is the kind of mountainous ter-rainthat for centuries was typical of most of Spain. Another landscape, much more familiar, comprises the rich basin of the River Guadalquivir, on the banks of which were constructed Seville itself, and the most important towns in the province . To the south, the country again becomes hilly, rising to the mountains of the Subetic Cordillera with the famous 'white villages' of the provinces of Málaga and Cádiz. Finally, to the south west, totally flat, the Guadalquivir winds its way to the sea, through the marsh-es of the Doñana National Park.

•**ERMITA DE CUATRO VITAS,** *Bollullos de la Mutación*
The Guadalquivir flows lazily (dropping scarcely 10 in 100m) through this cattle raising area at the edge of the marshes, on its way to the sea. There are many cortijos (large farmhouses), along the route of the Rocio. A curious survivor (above) is this 13th century Almohad minaret used as a chapel tower for the old hermitage.

• El Real de la Jara

Alnazcóllar•
Olivares• • Santiponce
Pilas•
Sevilla
A G
Bollullos de la Mitación

Utrera, Iglesia de Sta. María de la Mesa, with a Gothic interior and Renaissance façade.

The church of San Gil in Écija, a Gothic building of the 15th century., although the tower is Baroque like so many others in this,

'city of towers'. Like many other towns along via Augusta in the rich lowlands called the Campiña, Écija is a Roman foundation called by them Astigi. The Muslim town wall was built on top of the remains of the Roman.

•LA PUERTA DE CÓRDOBA, CARMONA
Although this is set in the reconstructed Roman city wall, this gate, through which passed the via Augusta, dates from the end of the 17th century. It has a martial flavour, more Neoclassical than Baroque.

•IGLESIA DE SAN JUAN BAUTISTA. *Écija*
This is Baroque, like almost all church towers in Écija. Built with just brick and tile work cleverly combined in intertwining designs and forms, giving an exhuberance of decoration almost Rococo.

•IGLESIA DE SAN PEDRO. CARMONA

The idea of the builders of this church of San Pedro was more to pay homage to the Giralda rather than immitate it, and it is thus called, 'la Giraldilla'. It was begun in the 15th century. with the tower added in the 17th. This contains all the elements and architectural forms which would give rise to the Neomudéjar style in the 20th century.

Badonlasa
Estepa
La Puebla de Cazalla
Osuna
Villanueva de San Juan
Montellano
Pruna

•CARMONA COUNTRYSIDE
This picture clearly shows the important role, from Romans to Muslims, played by agriculture in the fertile Campiña lowlands. From the heights of king Don Pedro's castle (now a Parador) the rich wheatfields, once the granary of Rome, stretch out of sight.

•Parador de Carmona

ⓘ **Tourist infor-
mation**
•Oficina de Turismo
*Puerta de Sevilla s/n
telf..95 595 36 26*

🏛 **Museum**

•Roman necropilis of
Carmona
*Avda de Jorge Bonsor, 9.
Telf. 95 414 08 11*

■ **Fiestas**

•Romería de la Virgen
de Gracia
September.

■ Carmona

This is an ancient town that is probably of Tartessian origin, although it was named by the Carthaginians, who called it "Kar-Hammon", in honour of their sun god. The Romans colonised it as "Carmo Romana"; we can still see the Amphitheatre and the remains of what was the Necropolis for over 600 years, where there are almost 800 tombs, of which only 250 have been excavated. Some of these, indeed, are entire villas, buried in the ground.

Also visi-

ble are parts of the wall around the town, including the impressive Seville Gate, altered in Arab times when

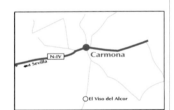

they fortified the town. It was a significant stronghold, with a high position overlooking the countryside, where abundant wheat was produced, just 40 km from Italica and bordering the Calzada, the Roman

road along which the wealth and civilisation of the

province was transported. A hundred years after the Chris-tian reconquest (1247), King Pedro I had a palace con-structed for his lover (with dungeons for his enemies) over the former Almohad Alcázar (fortress), known locally as 'the High Palace'. The splendid modern Parador (above) was built on the ruins of this palace. The old quarter of the town bears witness to the past with its many noble houses, church-es and convents.

•CHURCH OF SAN PEDRO. *Below left, the main square, Carmona.*

•FAÇADE *of a Baroque hermitage in Carmona*

- **ALCALÁ DE GUADAIRA.** *above.*
In Alcalá de Guadaira –literally 'fortress on the hill' – is this magnificent Almohad fortress with eight battlemented towers and constructed on top of a Roman fort. There is also a Roman bridge with seven spans, remodelled at the end of the 18th century.
Also to be seen are remains of Roman and Muslim flour mills which supplied Seville long before Alcalá became famous for its own bread.

■ **Écija.**

The modern motorway from Seville to Cordova follows the old Roman road.Along it, in a small depression alongside the river Genil (navigable from here seawards), is Écija, the 'Astigi' of the Romans.

Of the Muslim fortress, built on Roman remains, only two gates and four towers have survived.

The Lisbon earthquake of 1755 caused considerable damage in the town, but at a time when economic pros-

perity meant that this could be quickly repaired. Indeed, advantage was taken of the disaster to build grand and attractive new squares such

as the Plaza de España. This is popularly known as 'el Salón' (the sitting-room), a name which describes per-

fectly its public, yet familiar nature. Palaces, and churches were restored at the time, but above all the eleven towers which had suffered badly. They were rebuilt in a late Baroque style with local peculiarities based on the ingenious combination of colours and materials, chiefly brickwork and ceramic tiling. This gives the 'city of towers' its singular aspect. One could even speak of an 'Écija' style, with an influence well outside the region. Of the four palaces in the town, two, the Peñaflor, with its long façade and now a Parador, and the Vadehermoso, are the best examples of this mixture of styles and influences.

• **Plaza de España (el Salón). Écija the church of San Juan.**

ⓘ **Tourist Information**
Plza. de España. 1. telf. 95 590 29 33-19

• **Palacio de Peñaflor**
Emilio Castelar. 26. telf. 95 483 02 73

• **The Frying pan of Andalusia**
Sevillianos love nicknames and Ecija is popularly known as 'the frying pan of Andalusia', a graphic description of the soaring temperatures of August.

• *View of Estepa and, right, la Torre de la Victoria, almost 40m high and built in 1760, but with no church alongside.*

■ Estepa

This village in the province of Seville is famous for its 'mantecado' pastries, and lies on the slopes of the San Cristóbal ridge (above). The historian Titus Livy reported that in 207 BC the inhabitants of "Ostipo" chose to die rather than surrender to the Romans. From the "Balcony of Anda-lusia" at the top of the ridge, one can enjoy wonderful views of the undulating countryside. Here one can see the ruins of the walls and the Homage Tower, built by the Chrisians, overlooking the village.

Outstanding sights in the village include the Victory Tower (right), with its five brick storeys on a stone base, the church of the Assumption and the church of Carmen with a beautiful Baroque entrance of stone and black tiles.

■ Osuna

Osuna, too, stands on a hill overlooking the wide plain and is also of Iberian origin. It was conquered by the Ro-

mans, who called it "Urso" because of the bears that then inhabited the area. After

🏛 Museum

• **Archeológical Museum Padre Martín Recio.**
C/Ancha, 14. Telf. 95 591 40 88. Gratuito.

ⓘ Tourist Information
• **Oficina de Turismo**
Casa de la Cultura. 22. telf. 95 591 27 71

■ Fiestas

• *Romería, may*
• *Octava virgen de los Remedios*

the Romans, came the Moors and then the Christian Reconquest in the 13th century. The history of all these large villages of the Seville countryside is a similar one, reflecting the realities of conquest and colonisation.

When the Moors were pushed back to the Kingdom of Granada, Osuna was on the frontier with the Nasrid Kingdom, and controlled by the Calatrava Order, whose leader Téllez Girón was the force behind the growth of the town. In 1562, five generations later, and after the foundation of the University in 1548, the family was honoured with the title of Duchy of Osuna by King Philip II. Osuna became an important intellectual and artistic centre with

• MONASTERIO DE LA MERCED OR CONVENTO DE LA ENCARNACIÓN

•PALACIO DE LOS CONDES DE LA GOMERA.
•CILLA DEL CABILDO.
Below Windows

noble family palaces and churches. In 1967, it was declared a town of historical and artistic importance. The most important building is the Colegiata, which over-

looks the whole town. The collegiate church (1534) has three Renaissance aisles, a Baroque chancel and an east-facing Plateresque entrance. It contains paintings by Morales, a portrait of the Virgin by Alonso Cano and five youthful works by Ribera, including his famous Expiration of Christ and images of St Jerome, St Peter, St Bartholomew and St Sebastian over the altar and on some 16th century Flemish panels. There is a small Pantheon, the same age as the church, with three miniature intricately-

worked aisles, and containing a family crypt. The Encarnación monastery was originally a hospital and transformed into a convent in the 17th century. It possesses one of the most beautiful towers in all Andalusia, as well as a cloister containing a museum, and socles with painted tiles. The street called San Pedro has been described as the most important Baroque monumental complex in all Andalusia; the outstanding buildings are the Cilla del Cabildo and the Palace of the Marquesses of la Go-

•**ANTIGUA CILLA** *del cabildo (the Old Cilla).*

🏛 MUSEUMS

•**MUSEO ARQUEOLÓGICO. TORRE DEL AGUA.**
C/ San Antón, s/n telf., 95 481 12 07. (Osuna)

•**MONASTERIO DE LA ENCARNACIÓN.**
Plza. de la Encarnación, 2. telf. 95 481 11 21.

• **MUSEO DE ARTE SACRO**
Iglesia colegial de la Villa. Extramuros. Telf. 95 481 04 44

① TOURIST INFORMATION

•**OFICINA DE TURISMO**
Casa de la Cultura. 22. telf. 95 481 22 58

•**AYUNTAMIENTO**

FIESTAS

•**VIRGEN DE LA CONSO-LACIÓN**
Fiestas patronales (Osuna). 8th september.

•**FERIA DE MAYO**

•**FIESTAS PATRONALES DE SAN ARCADIO (JANUARY)**

● SANTUARIO DE CUATROVITAS

This is a small rural hermitage. The tower was the former minaret of a 13th century Almohad mosque built, somewhat suprisingly, out in the country.

🏛 MUSEUM

● ERMITA DE CUATROVITAS.

ⓘ TOURIST INFORMATION

● AYUNTAMIENTO
954 76 50 00

FIESTAS

● virgen de cuatrovitas
● corpus christi
● feria (septiembre)

■ BOLLULLOS DE LA MITACIÓN AND EL ROCÍO

Bollullos is a small village 12km south-west of Seville in which is one of the few surviving rural Almohad (13th century) 'rabitas' or hermitages (above). It is on the borderlands of the great marshes, just up river from the villages of Coria, La Puebla and Los Palacios. All of them are on the route to El Rocío, the extraordinary fiesta-pilgrimage in the marsh village with which Seville is closely identified. As with so many other Christian festivals, El Rocío has its roots in pagan ceremonies, in this case the celebration of Spring and the unique cattle rearing life on the marsh. In historical terms

it can be dated back to at least the 13th century when Alfonso X, the Wise, built the hermitage of Santa María de las Rocinas. The miraculous descovery of a statue of the Virgin in the 15th century bolstered the Marian tradition and reinforced popular devotion. In the 17th century a few thousand made the pilgrimage, but nowadays it is a phenomenon of the masses, unique and difficult for an outsider to understand.

■ Italica

Publius Cornelus Scipio, 'the African', fo
Itálica for his retired veterans after w
the second Punic War in 206 BC. It w
first Roman city built in Spain. In time t
became one of the most important
Empire, especially after AD 53 whe
emperor Trajan was born here. He was later to choose another man born
Hadrian, to succeed him as emperor. This last gave the city the title of 'c
and richly endowed it with the greater part of what has come down to
is less certain if Theodosius was born here, but he was the last emperor
an active interest in glorifying the city.

THE HOUSE OF BIRDS
A mosaic with masterly representation of 32
ent species of birds.

• **TRAJAN** *was the real*
dinamo of the city which
his successor Hadrian,
like Augustus a grand
empire builder, made a
colony and richly
endowed with all sorts of

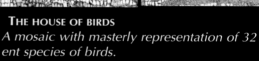

• **ENGRAVING**
ITÁLICA
For centurie
especially ir
Romantic ag
the 19th cer
Itálica has b
an inspiratio
poets and ot
writers for th
beauty of its
Less agreeab
reading of th
graphic acco
of despoliati
the same ce

HE AMPHITHEATRE AT ITÁLICA. *This was one of the biggest in the Roman world, with* ɔacity *for an audience of 25,000. It is elliptical in plan and measures 160m. x* ⁷m. *and gives a clear idea of what the size of the population must have been.* ny *of the statues which adorned it are now in museums.*

•THE MOSAICS (ABOVE, NEPTUNE)

The importance of this town is also reflected in the streets that are 15 metres wide (those of Pompeii were only 10 metres wide) and their magnificent mosaics which, though some were plundered over the centuries, remain eloquent reminders of past grandeur.

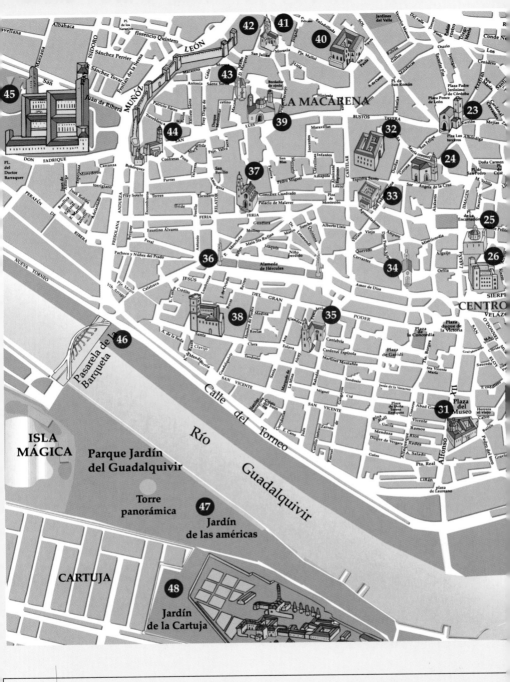

Key to plan

1. Catedral y Giralda
2. Palacio Arzobispal
3. Convento de la Encarnación
4. Iglesia de Santa Cruz
5. Iglesia de Santa María la Blanca
6. Hospital de los Venerables
7. Reales Alcázares
8. Archivo de Indias
9. Hospital de la Caridad
10. Teatro de la Maestranza
11. Plza de Toros de la Maestranza
12. Torre del Oro
13. Puente de Isabel II
14. Iglesia de San Jacinto
15. Iglesia de Santa Ana
16. Palacio de San Telmo
17. Universidad
18. Casino de la Exposición
19. Plaza de España
20. Iglesia de San Esteban
21. Iglesia de San Ildefonso
22. Iglesia de San Nicolás
23. Iglesia de Santa Catalina
24. Iglesia de San Pedro
25. Iglesia de la Anunciación
26. Palacio de Lebrija

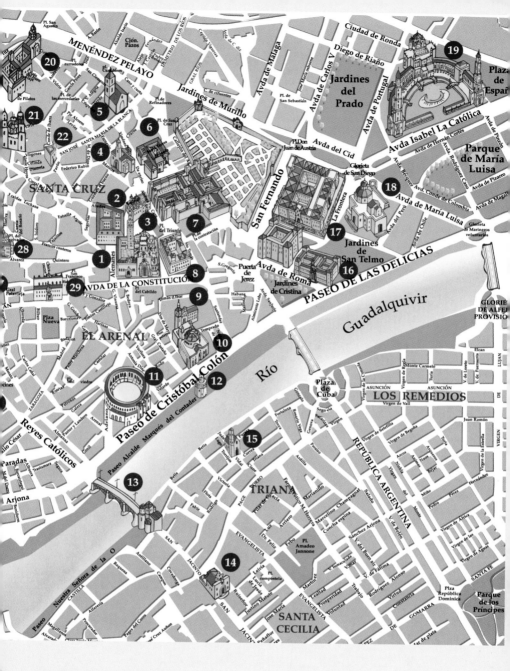

27. Iglesia de San José
28. Iglesia del Salvador
29. Ayuntamiento
30. Iglesia de la Magdalena
31. Museo de Bellas Artes
32. Casa Palacio de las Dueñas
33. Convento del Espíritu Santo
34. Iglesia de San Andrés
35. Iglesia de San Lorenzo

y Jesús del Gran Poder
36. Alameda de Hércules
37. Iglesia Omnium Sanctorum
38. Convento de Santa Clara
y Torre de Don Fadrique
39. Iglesia de San Luis
40. Convento de Santa Paula
41. Iglesia de San Julián
42. Murallas
43. Iglesia de Santa Marina

44. Iglesia de San Gil
45. Hospital de las Cinco
Llagas
46. Puente de la Barqueta
47. Auditorio de la Cartuja
48. Monasterio de
Santa María de las Cuevas